CHRISTINA
AGUILERA

CHRISTINA AGUILERA

LISA DEGNEN

MetroBooks

An Imprint of Friedman/Fairfax Publishers

© 2000 by Michael Friedman Publishing Group, Inc.

Library of Congress Cataloging-in-Publication Data

Degnen, Lisa.
    Christina Aguilera / by Lisa Degnen.
        p.cm.
    Includes bibliograpohical references (p.) and index.
    ISBN 1-58663-036-9 (alk. paper)
    1. Aguilera, Christina, 1980- 2. Singers—United States—
    Biography. I. Title.

    ML420 .A337 D44 2000
    782.42164'092—dc21
    [B]
        00-033226

Editors: Ann Kirby and Dan Heend
Art Director: Jeff Batzli
Designer: Mark Weinberg
Photography Editors: Kathleen Wolfe, Erin Feller

Color separations by Radstock Repro
Printed in England by Butler & Tanner Ltd.

10 9 8 7 6 5 4 3 2 1

For bulk purchases and special sales, please contact:
Friedman/Fairfax Publishers
Attention: Sales Department
15 West 26th Street
New York, NY 10010
212/685-6610 FAX 212/685-1307

Visit our website:
www.metrobooks.com

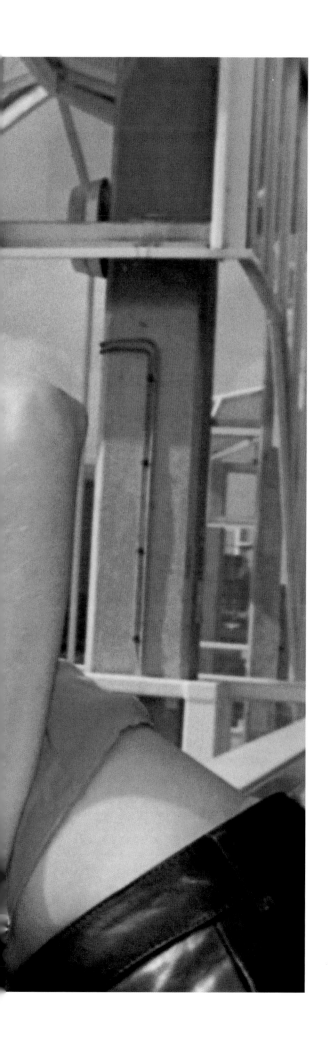

Contents

CHAPTER ONE

Christina Takes on the World

"I'm a very spiritual person. I have a strong belief in God, who has completely led me to this point," Christina says. "There were days years ago when I wanted fame more than anything in this entire world, and I would pray so hard."

Christina says her greatest artistic influences growing up were Whitney Houston, Mariah Carey, and Etta James. One of the biggest thrills of her life was when critics started calling her "the new Mariah."

Christina Aguilera's life has been one endless dream come true. By the age of nineteen, she had already seen and done more than many people do in a lifetime—and achieved a level of success that some performers never reach.

FAMILY TIES

Christina has always known she wanted to be a star. Her Ecuadoran-born father, Fausto, and his Irish-American wife, Shelly, originally lived on New York City's Staten Island, where their first daughter, Christina, was born. Christina's dad was in the military, and her mom was a violinist and pianist who had toured Europe with the Youth Symphony Orchestra in her teens. So adventure and performing were in Christina's blood. As a little girl, she was already the star

ABOVE: Christina is enjoying every moment of her success. She certainly has a lot to smile at these days... like being one of the most popular artists in the country.

OPPOSITE: "I'm half Irish, half Latina," Christina says of her roots. "My father is from Ecuador."

PREVIOUS PAGES: *On January 4th, Christina was thrilled to find out she was nominated for a Grammy as Best New Artist. It was the best day of her life—until she won, of course!*

BELOW: *Christina's mom, Shelly, and her sisters, Stephanie and Rachel, are always there to support her. "They are so great," Christina says with a smile.*

OPPOSITE: *Christina loves experimenting with great new looks.*

of the family. "She would surround herself with stuffed animals and they'd be her audience," her mom says.

The army sent Fausto to a different post every few months, so Christina lived all over the world as a little girl, from Japan to Florida to New Jersey to Texas.

When Christina was five years old, her parents divorced and she moved with her mom and her younger sister, Rachel, to Wexford, a suburb of Pittsburgh. Eventually her mother married a paramedic named James Kearns, who has become more of a father to Christina than Fausto, whom she hardly ever sees. And even though she now has an apartment in New York City and engagements all over the world, Christina still calls Wexford home. When she takes a break from touring, she looks forward to savoring relaxing moments there. "All I want for Christmas is to be home, to do all the things I used to do before things exploded," she smiles. "I want to play video games with my brothers and sisters and open presents."

A STAR IN THE MAKING

When she was just eight years old, Christina started appearing regularly in talent shows and even performed on the national television show *Star Search.* "I wanted to perform as long as I could remember," admits the blue-eyed beauty. Eventually, at the ripe old age of ten, she was singing the national anthem for the Pittsburgh Steelers and Penguins.

By the time she was twelve, Christina was practically a show-business veteran. She landed a role on the *Mickey Mouse Club* and moved to Orlando to perform on the show that also featured pop-stars-to-be Britney Spears, JC Chasez, and Justin Timberlake. One reviewer has described the show as a sort of "Pop Stars for Dummies," a proving ground on which rising stars learn the ropes of performing before going on to successful careers.

Christina says being on the set was actually like being at a summer camp. "I was there for two seasons with Britney Spears and Justin and JC from 'N Sync," Christina remembers. "We all became like brothers and sisters. . . . Britney

"When I see all these peo-ple screaming and chanting and holding up signs that they made just for me, my eyes light up, my whole body lifts and I feel like I'm in another state," Christina explains.

Christina's Vital Stats

Full name: **Christina Maria Aguilera**

Birthdate: **December 18, 1980**

Star sign: **Sagittarius**

Birthplace: **Staten Island, New York**

Height: **5 feet 2 inches (157.5cm)**

Hair: **Blonde**

Eyes: **Blue**

Hometown: **Wexford, Pennsylvania**

Current home: **New York City**

Parents: **Shelly** and **Fausto;**
    stepfather **James Kearns**

Siblings: sister **Rachel**, stepbrother **Michael**,
    stepsister **Stephanie**, half-brother **Casey**

Pets: **Fozzie the dog, Tiger the cat**

Favorite colors: **Turquoise, fuschia**

Favorite foods: **Bacon cheeseburgers,
    chili cheese fries**

Favorite performers: **Mariah Carey, Madonna,
    Enrique Iglesias, Whitney Houston,
    Michael Jackson, Brian McKnight,
    Julie Andrews, Etta James**

Favorite sports: **Baseball, volleyball**

Favorite actors: **Johnny Depp, Ben Affleck**

Favorite subjects in school: **English, science**

Favorite designer: **Dolce & Gabbana**

Where to write to her:
    Christina Aguilera Fan Club
    244 Madison Avenue, Suite 314
    New York, NY 10016
    E-mail: fanmail@christinamail.com

"I actually had no real training in dancing or vocals," says Christina. "When I did the *Mickey Mouse Club*, there was an on-set choreographer and a vocal coach, so they both helped me expand my own instincts."

RIGHT: Christina's mom Shelly says that when Christina was a kid, she would often perform for her stuffed animals if there was no one else to listen to her—not that she'll ever have to worry about that again!

ABOVE: "Sometimes I'm singing in my daydream," Christina says. *"When I have a hard day, I explore this whole imaginary side of my brain."*

and I were the youngest, and we totally looked up to the older kids, especially Keri Russell, who was fifteen."

Keri Russell went on to big television fame on WB's *Felicity.* But before all that, she too was a Mouseketeer! "She was the first one to fray her jeans, which was really cool at the time," Christina recalls. "And she was so beautiful, we were just in awe of her."

The show was Christina's first really big break, but it didn't come right away. She was too young to join the cast her first try. "There was an open audition for *Mickey Mouse Club* in Pittsburgh when I was nine, but I didn't get picked." The producers didn't forget about her, however. "They asked me back later, though, and I was eventually chosen to be a presenter when I was twelve," she says. "It was a really great experience."

Still, she wasn't thrilled with some of the antics that the show's producers came up with. "I had a pie thrown in my face," she remembers. "That wasn't too much fun."

The show also caused her some problems at home from jealous kids, who didn't like the idea of the girl next door suddenly becoming a television star. "They'd be like, 'Who does she think she is?'" she says. "I couldn't have a bad day like other kids, because everyone looks at you and says, 'Ha, I told you she was like that!' It makes you grow up faster, but it makes you stronger, too."

"Going to a public school in a small town and not being around kids who did what I did made me feel like an outsider. I even had to switch elementary schools after I went on *Star Search*. The jealousy

got really bad. People just felt threatened. . . . Kids didn't know how to deal with seeing their peer on television. You learn the hard way who your friends are. Plus my circle of friends was the cheerleading clique and there was already a lot of backstabbing."

After two years with the Disney show, Christina traveled overseas to further hone her musical skills and establish herself as an international star. She recorded a duet, "All I Wanna Do," with Japanese pop star Keizo Nakanishi, and she toured Asia and Europe. All over the world, Christina was a hit. When she waded into the crowd at the Golden Stag Festival in Transylvania, Romania (the home of Dracula), to perform just two songs, she caused a near riot. Amazingly, Christina—who was fairly unknown at the time—got even more attention than her famous costars, Sheryl Crow and Diana Ross. And that was just the beginning.

"Just seeing my name at No. 1 on a Billboard chart—it's always been a dream," Christina says.

"Hopefully when I'm onstage, I'm touching kids on a level that other people don't," Christina says.

CHAPTER TWO

Christina Out of the Bottle

"When I open my mouth, people are still surprised by what comes out," says five-foot-two-inch Christina. "But don't under-estimate—big things come in small packages."

On stage she's a star, but off stage she says she's just like any other girl. "When I go home to see my family, I look forward to doing real stuff," Christina says.

With the Mickey Mouse Club and an international single already under her belt, Christina was ready to take on the pop charts back home in the United States. Coincidentally, her first big music success would come from Disney, but this time, she'd be singing for the silver screen.

CHRISTINA'S "REFLECTION"

When Christina returned home to the United States in 1998, she was given the opportunity to audition for Disney, who was looking for a girl with a powerful voice to record the song "Reflection" for the movie *Mulan*. At her manager's suggestion, Christina cut a one-take demo on the boom box in her living room, singing along with a karaoke tape of Whitney Houston's "I Wanna Run to You." Disney was

ABOVE: Christina says that she will always remember her days as a Mouseketeer. "I had a following of fans who stuck with me from The Mickey Mouse Club," *Christina says. "Disney played a big part in helping me to break my career."*

OPPOSITE: Christina's blonde hair and blue eyes — plus her amazing singing abilities—made her an instant pinup princess.

Christina vs. Britney: Is There Really a Feud Between the Two Stars?

For a long time now, people have been talking about how much the two *Mickey Mouse Club* alumni hate each other and each other's music. Christina says nothing could be further from the truth. "We were really close, really good friends," she says. "When the *Mickey Mouse Club* ended, in which we starred, we went our separate ways." But that doesn't mean they parted as anything other than friends; in fact, Christina says that the duo may even record a single together soon.

Christina says that when Britney first found success, everyone who first knew her from her *Mickey Mouse Club* days was thrilled. "When Britney's album was about to come out, I thought about calling radio stations to request her song," she says. "Then she blew up and I was like, 'She doesn't need me.'" She adds, "[Britney] deserves her success, she's really hardworking. I've always known her to be a really sweet girl."

Christina does admit that she does find it a little irritating when people are constantly comparing her to Britney or calling her the "new" Britney. "It's frustrating," Christina says. "We are two different artists and it wouldn't be an issue if we weren't the same age and from the same kind of background. It's because we seem so

much alike." She adds, "It's most frustrating when the fans compare us. My mom runs my fan club and she'll be reading certain things and it's the catfighting between some fans which is really frustrating."

However, both Christina and Britney seem to realize that as they become more established, the public is beginning to recognize their distinct styles and personalities. "Now," Christina says, "people are starting to realize Britney and I are two completely different artists. We both sing and dance but I'm newer and she's well established. More people compare me with Mariah Carey now."

In fact, the two stars are different in just about every way, from their tastes in boys to clothes and music. When Britney was on the cover of *Rolling Stone* magazine, she wore a skimpy bikini and held a Teletubby—definitely not a move Christina would make. "If I was on the cover, I'd pose in something genie-ish and sexy," she says with a smile. "And instead of a Teletubby, maybe I'll pose with Robbie Williams."

When Britney is asked if she thinks Christina is riding on her coattails, she is also good-natured and diplomatic. "I don't think it's a matter of someone stealing my thunder," Britney says. "It's about hard work and determination. Christina's got it and she'll do really well."

Christina (second from the right) and Britney (seated on the floor) before they were stars, posing with the rest of the cast of The New Mickey Mouse Club.

Christina says she loves living in her new New York City apartment. "I'm really getting used to it," she says. "When I moved from Pittsburgh to make my record in L.A., I lived out of a hotel. So it feels a little strange having my own place now and shopping for myself."

blown away by her performance, and immediately signed her up to record their song. At the time, RCA Records was about to sign Christina to a recording contract. It was an amazing week.

Mulan premiered in June 1998 and "Reflection" quickly landed on the charts, eventually cracking the top fifteen on the adult contemporary list. Performing live on television shows like *CBS This Morning* and the *Donny & Marie Show,* Christina got her first taste of what it was really like to be famous, and got a chance to make audiences across the United States familiar with her incredible voice and stunning face. "The song's theme—the struggle to establish your identity—was something I could really relate to as a teenage girl myself," she said. Christina was thrilled when the song received a Golden Globe nomination for Best Original Song in a Motion Picture.

LAYING DOWN TRACKS

Meanwhile, Christina was hard at work on her self-titled debut album for RCA. The album took a while to produce and the process was full of ups and downs, but she was lucky to be working with some of the biggest names in the business, including David Frank and Steve Kipner, who wrote "The Hardest Thing" for 98 Degrees; Diane Warren, who wrote Aerosmith's Grammy-nominated "I Don't Want to Miss a Thing" among other mega-hits; and Carl Stunken and Evan Rogers, who have produced numerous hits for 'N Sync. Although Christina didn't write any of the songs herself, she looks forward to having a few Christina originals on future albums!

The record taps into every side of her musical personality and her fantastic voice. "Genie in a Bottle" is fun, "What a Girl Wants" covers her romantic side, "So Emotional" has gospel overtones, and the ballad "I Turn to You" talks about finding your own way as you grow up. Fueled by the success of the first single released in June 1999, "Genie in a Bottle," the album ended up being so hot that it debuted at number one on the *Billboard* charts in August. Selling 253,000 in its first week, the album even outsold the long-

PREVIOUS PAGES: *Before she was a star, Christina says that she tried everything that she thought might help her become famous. "I always wished on my birthday and I've thrown loads of pennies in fountains at the mall, too! I wished on a star back in my home town, hoping I'd be one myself one day!"*

awaited Puff Daddy *Forever* album by more than 50,000 copies. It also blew Britney Spears' first album right out of the water. Britney's album sold only 120,000 copies in its first week!

"Genie in a Bottle" was quickly put into heavy rotation on MTV and on radio stations and in dance clubs around the world, but not without a bit of undue controversy. There have been times when the dynamic blond singer can't believe she has to defend the song that turned her into a star, but she says there's been a lot of misunderstanding. She firmly believes it is a song with a message to young girls that they have to believe in themselves and not let other people walk all over them. She denies that it has the suggestive message for which some have criticized it.

"In the past, a genie has always been portrayed as a slave for a man," she explains. "But in my song, we've changed it around. It's like, `I'm not coming out of my bottle until you do what I want!' I make the wishes come true

LEFT: Christina gets close with Mark McGrath of Sugar Ray while presenting an award.

OPPOSITE: Christina says that she wants to be a little controversial and a little unpredictable. "I always want to shock people throughout my career," she says. "Like Madonna."

too. . . . It's a total girl-powerful song."

The second single from *Christina Aguilera*, "What a Girl Wants," is another song about female empowerment. It's one of Christina's favorite songs. "It's about a girl who is a little unsure," she explains. "She has maybe been hurt before. She needs her space. She needs her time to figure out who she is. She needs her independence. And this guy who's been there from the beginning— he gives her everything that she's ever needed, whether it be space, or time, or love and affection, until she has time to find herself." When the girl is finally ready to start the relationship, Christina explains, this guy is ready and waiting to "give her what a girl wants."

And also like "Genie," it was an outrageous success. "What a Girl Wants" became the first number-one single of the new century! It seems as if everything this genie puts her hands on turns to gold—or platinum, as the success of *Christina Aguilera* has proved.

OPPOSITE: Christina has taken her fashion forward cues from other pop stars. "I look up to the greats, the experimental people themselves— Madonna, Janet Jackson—who always have something new and creative to offer to the public," she says.

RIGHT: Christina loves getting dressed up and looked amazing at the MTV Awards in Dublin, Ireland.

"There were days when I wanted fame more than anything in this entire world, and I would pray so hard," Christina says. Prayers are obviously answered some of the time, because Christina has more than she ever dreamed of.

CHAPTER THREE

The Sky's the Limit

"I tend to be a control freak and a perfectionist," Christina says. "I think that's what drives me, because it gives me control over a situation. I hate feeling vulnerable."

"There are definitely down sides to stardom,"
Christina says. "I missed out on the whole
going to school thing with my friends,
going to football games, going to the prom.
But if I was sitting in school right now,
I'd probably be looking out the widow
fantasizing about the life I'm living now."

Christina didn't become a superstar from her hit album alone. Even after the record hit the top of the charts, there was more work to be done. With touring, making videos, traveling, a trip to the Grammy podium, and an eye toward the recording studio, Christina has been building even more momentum, ensuring that her star will continue to rise.

2000: THE YEAR OF CHRISTINA

It's been quite a year of accolades for this amazing new star. Not long after her first album, *Christina Aguilera,* was released, she appeared on *The Tonight Show* with Jay Leno and on the *Back to School Bash* television show, all while "Genie" was screaming up the charts. And the readers of *Teen People* named her best new artist. "With all the new talented artists out there," Christina responded, "I am honored to have been chosen number one by the readers and fans."

Christina performed with Toni Braxton and Enrique Iglesias in front of literally millions of fans at Super Bowl XXXII, furthering her status as a household name. She also

ABOVE: "I'm always traveling and I'm always on the road," Christina says. "Sometimes it's hard to meet people for more than two seconds. It's really difficult. I'm sure I'll meet that special guy somehow on the road."

OPPOSITE: Christina vamping it up for the cameras at the 1999 Alma Awards.

Presenting Miss Aguilera

At the MTV video awards in September 1999, Christina presented the award for Best Rock Video, which Korn took home for "Freak on a Leash." She was accompanied to the podium by rock bad-boy Tommy Lee, former Motley Crue drummer and perhaps best known as the on-again, off-again husband of blonde bombshell Pamela Anderson.

"We were really nervous at first," said Tommy Lee, who was dressed in a raincoat and seemingly nothing else. "I talked her down. I was like, it's okay, it's okay. . . I could tell she was shy. She's cute."

Christina agrees that having wildman Tommy Lee by her side actually made the whole nerve-wracking experience a little easier. "He helped me," she laughs. "He's more experienced than I am. . . . And we just met, and I was too shy to introduce myself. He was first. He was like, 'Hi, I'm Tommy. Nice to meet you.'"

OPPOSITE: Christina says she has always wanted to sing, but she has her grandmother to thank for starting her career.

RIGHT: Tommy Lee and Christina at the 1999 MTV Music Video Awards.

ON TOUR

Christina's very first experience as a touring artist came when she jumped on the road with T-boz, Chili, and Left Eye of TLC in January 2000. Just like everything else that was happening to her at the moment, the experience made Christina feel like she was living in a dream world. She had been waiting for this moment her entire life and now she couldn't believe everything was coming true.

"I would watch the home videos of Janet Jackson and Madonna and there were always just so many different fans and everything, and to feel like a little level of that, it's just like, wow!" she says. "It's really cool, I was really looking forward to getting out there and experiencing it."

Christina said that performing in front of live crowds night after night has proven to be as fulfilling as she had anticipated. "It was all about the live performances and playing these venues and hearing the kids. I mean, hearing kids sing back to me my own lyrics is something I've always wanted."

GENIE ON FILM?

Christina has become more than just a singer. As anyone who's seen her videos can attest, she is really comfortable in front of a camera, and she looks stunningly beautiful. Indeed, directors have been flocking to ask her to appear in their movies, but Christina has decided that a glamorous movie career will have to wait. "Right now, I'm continuing to focus on my singing," says Christina. "I've been waiting for this moment my whole life." She is still involved in the movie business though, having contributed a song, "Don't Make Me Love You," to the soundtrack for the Madonna–Rupert Everett flick, *The Next Best Thing*.

Christina believes strongly in women's rights.
"Right now I'm reading Reviving Ophelia *by Mary Pipher," she says. "It's really opened my eyes and reinforced how important it is to be confident and believe in yourself no matter what anyone says."*

A music career isn't all that Christina dreams of. "I'd like to pursue acting once I'm more established as a recording artist," she says. "But singing is my first love."

Christina's Big Scare

Christina Aguilera was going to go out and do a simple autograph signing at a Target store in Pasadena, California, but she said it turned out to be "one of the scariest moments of my life."

More than two thousand fans turned up at the mall, many with their parents. Some of them had been waiting in line for up to eight hours and they were tired and angry by the time she arrived.

"You could just feel this crowd of people," Christina says. "It became like this stampede, and I was really worried that a lot of little kids would get hurt." Christina says that she was really surprised to see how many people had turned out to see her. Suddenly, though, the shoving started. "People were sort of getting out of hand, pushing and whatnot," Christina says. "We weren't expecting that many people to come up. Target has had a lot of other groups, including 'N Sync and The Backstreet Boys and they never had a problem before. So it was really odd that something like that had happened. I guess the store just got too packed."

"It was really scary because I was barricaded off with all these policemen around me and I've never felt that way before," Christina says. "It just became overwhelming, all the people. I mean there were people climbing the shelves to get a better look!"

Luckily, the local police ultimately did a good job of handling the situation. "Fortunately, everything was fine," she says. "No one was hurt. . . . It was just a scary thing to go through, and I know it has shaken up some people. I just think in the future we'll take better security precautions to ensure that maybe these things are better organized and to expect the worst."

"I've got my own apartment in New York and I want to decorate it, but I haven't been able to put my personality into it yet," says busy Christina. "But I'm totally into deco-rating, even when I was younger I used to play with my Barbies and I would spend ages decorating their house then never play with them again."

PREVIOUS PAGES: Beyond being a forum for displaying her obvious vocal talents and belting out her chart-topping songs, Christina's live performances afford her the opportunity to show off some energetic and imaginative choreography.

LONELY AT THE TOP

As happy as she is to be successful, Christina has discovered there's a price to pay for letting her "Genie in a Bottle" out. Ever since she's had a hit single, she hasn't had a boyfriend.

Christina thought she finally had it all after years of struggling to get to the top. But when "Genie in a Bottle" topped the charts, Christina knew she was really a star. And now—when every guy in the world would like nothing more than to go out on a date with her—she is practically unavailable, since her schedule keeps her constantly on the go, touring, singing, and signing autographs.

"Traveling can get very lonely," she confesses, "staying in all these hotel rooms every night without having a sense of a real home base." The sometimes grueling schedule can take its toll, she explains. "It's really exhausting and the schedule's really tough. Everybody tried to warn me about this before I came out and I was like, `I don't care.' I just wanted to do it, do it, do it. Nothing could have prepared me for this."

And as physically exhausting as the work can be, she says often the emotional cost is even worse. She describes the drain of promoting a record: "Give, give, give all the time—whether it's with press, to your record label, or fans. Suddenly it's all over and it's time to go back by yourself."

Christina admits she sometimes dreams that she had a romantic guy to come home to. "I want affection and it's not there," she says sadly. "I meet a lot of guys on the road who give me marriage proposals and whatnot. But as far as a serious relationship, it's really hard to have, considering the fact that I'm always traveling. Sometimes it's hard to meet people more than two seconds. It's really difficult. I'm sure I'll meet that special guy somehow on the road."

But before you start to feel too sorry for her, you might like to know that Christina had not one but two dates to her

LEFT: "I travel a lot, and when I returned halfway through the school year, some people welcomed me," she says. "Others assumed I was a snob, which really hurt."

high school prom! At first Christina asked a girlfriend to hook her up on a blind date with "a really cute guy." But at the same time, there was another guy who really wanted to take her. "A friend of mine was hurt because he wanted to go with me, so I ended up with two dates," she laughs.

But even with more dates than many people get in a year, Christina says the night definitely had a dark side. "Only two girls came up to talk to me," she says. "Later I found out they were telling their boyfriends, 'If you talk to her, I'll kill you.'" Christina doesn't like it when girls try to compete with each other. She believes that girls should love themselves and each other.

"My album's actually very positive and spiritual," she says. "I want to convey a good message to young girls. Songs like 'Reflection' are really good for young girls because it's about finding yourself and learning to love yourself. It's about positivity."

LEFT: *"There is a special guy back home, and he'll always be special to me," Christina says. But we can't get her to reveal that special guy's name!*

OPPOSITE: *She's a Genie in a Bottle, baby!*

CHAPTER FOUR

¡Hola Christina!

"I definitely think there should be more female producers," says Christina. "I've noticed that some female artists, like Lauryn Hill, go to produce for other artists, but I can't think of many full-time producers who are female. It makes me want to be one myself."

Christina says she's just an average girl. "Society has created this image of the perfect girl," she says. "Lots of times we buy into that, to the point where we don't feel good about ourselves. It's my mission to change that whole mindset."

RIGHT: "I always work hard, but sometimes things just fall in my lap," Christina says. "I think everyone's meant to do or be a certain thing in life. The way I see it, what's meant to happen, will, so don't worry about it—there's no point!"

By mid-2000, Christina Aguilera was already so hot that if you got too close to her you'd probably catch on fire. Her self-titled first album had sold upward of four million copies; she'd nailed the coveted Grammy Award for Best New Artist; and she had performed for millions of people at the Super Bowl. But instead of just sitting back and basking in the glory, Christina decided that the success she'd already achieved was only the beginning.

"Everything is going great so far," she laughs. "It's all about using my creativity and exploring all facets of the business." By the time

RIGHT: Christina says the coolest part of her job is performing in front of an audience. "I really love being onstage; it's like home to me," she explains.

¡Hola Christina!

the din of applause from her Grammy win had begun to fade, Christina was already working on her next project.

EXPLORING HER LATIN ROOTS

Christina's father is Ecuadoran, and even though she doesn't speak a lot of Spanish yet, she's busy learning so that she can record in Spanish for her next album. Her mom, who used to be a translator, has encouraged Christina to get in touch with her roots.

"I can't speak Spanish as well as I can understand it, but I'm working on it," she says. "My parents separated [when I was] at a young age, but the culture was a big part of my childhood. Making the album is something I've always wanted to do, and it should come naturally because I've got a feel for the music."

With Christina's background and incredible voice, it seems likely that the new Spanish album will be a hit. Already she has gained exposure to a wider audience, appearing on the cover of *Latin Girl* magazine.

OPPOSITE: *"It's like I'm floating on air,"*
Christina says of her wonderful career.

RIGHT: *Christina says the only time she really feels like a star is when she turns up for award shows like Teen Choice. "Getting out of the limo and getting interviewed with fans all around cheering— it's when I feel like a real celebrity!"*

Get to Know Christina

IF SHE HAD THREE WISHES: "I want a driver's license, and the second wish would be a little sports car, and the third . . . five more wishes!"

HOBBIES: Christina just likes doing "regular" things that she rarely has the time to do anymore. She told *Jump* magazine in September 1999, "When I go home to see my family, I look forward to doing real stuff—scraping my knees, getting my clothes dirty, and fishing with my girlfriends. It's easy to get spoiled on the road. Being around my family keeps me in check."

REGRETS: "I was home-schooled my senior year, so I didn't get to walk down the aisle with a tasseled cap and I've never had my picture in the yearbook. I'm a little bummed about that."

BIGGEST TURN-OFF: "I'd hate to be stuck in an elevator with someone with bad body odor!"

FAVORITE BOOK: *Reviving Ophelia* by Mary Pipher. "It's really opened my eyes and reinforced how important it is to be confident and believe in yourself no matter what anyone says," Christina says.

WORST MOMENT: When she went to her then-boyfriend's high school prom in Pittsburgh. Christina says all the other girls gave her icy stares and when the DJ started playing "Genie

OPPOSITE: Christina says she'd love to tour with her dream guy. "I'd like to tour with Robbie Williams, but he can't open for me, he's too famous!," she says.

ABOVE: Christina says becoming a famous singer wasn't really a career choice. "I don't think I even decided," she says. "My love for this alone has carried me to where I am now."

ABOVE: Christina says even though she's always traveling, there are still places she would like to see. "I've never been to Ecuador," she says. "I just want to see the whole world."

OPPOSITE: Christina practices her moves in preparation for another well-choreographed and exciting live performance.

in a Bottle," they all left the dance floor. "It was kind of sad," she says.

FAVORITE CHARITIES: Christina thinks the fight against domestic violence is really important. "I saw certain things growing up that really affected me," she says. "It's too easy to give in to peer pressure, to listen too much to the male's opinion. I receive letters from fans writing about certain abusive situations that they are in, and that is why I want to reach out."

SPECIAL MOMENTS: Of course, ever since her singing career took off, Christina has had almost too many great experiences to remember. One of the best was ringing in the new millennium in New York's Times Square with her friends from MTV. "I've grown up watching the ball go down in Times Square. It's been `Omigod, I want to be there one day.' And then I was!"

SECRET TATTOO: Christina has a secret tattoo of Mickey Mouse somewhere on her body—and she's not telling where!

GOALS: To be the best singer she can be and move into acting, while still continuing as a singer. She also wants to visit South America, and to learn to speak Spanish, and to play the piano. "I really want to take piano lessons now," she says, "because it would help me so much when I write songs."

WHAT'S NEXT

Christina is also working on a Christmas album and even hoping to get into acting. "It's definitely sad that a lot of people don't know me as a vocalist," she explains. "But the more singles I release will hopefully make people start to realize there's more to my music and my voice than just being a teen pop star with catchy songs."

Christina says that even though she's on top now, she doesn't want to feel that she's got to be at the top if she's not producing great tunes. "There's always pressure," she says. "Naturally, I put pressure on myself to keep going further because it's all about record sales. So it does get crazy." But she doesn't take her success for granted. "It's all been pretty unbelievable so far," she smiles. "I'm having a very, very, very good time!"

OPPOSITE: "There are people around me that are definitely giving me love and support and affection," Christina says. "But right now, my career is my boyfriend."

LEFT: Christina looking dazzling at the American Teacher Awards.

Christina says that being in a tough business like the music industry has made her more mature. "If you are in a business where everyone is twenty years your senior," she says, "you have to work harder to get your points across and be heard. It's been difficult, but I intend to be in this business for a long time."

70

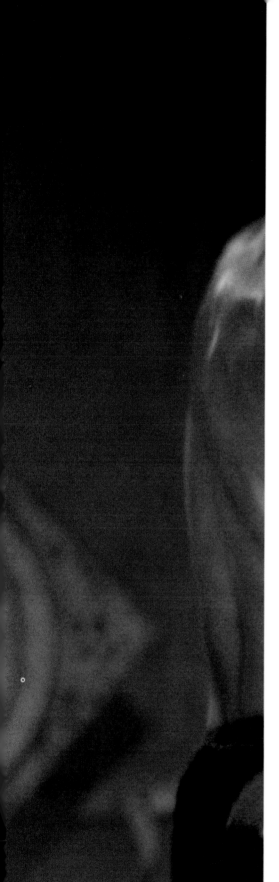

CHAPTER FIVE

Christina Style

"She can definitely dance," says choreographer Jermaine Brown, who put all the moves together for the "Genie" video. "Whatever I threw at her, she went along with it."

"When I did The Mickey Mouse Club *there was an on-set choreographer and a vocal coach, so they both helped me expand my own instincts," says Christina.*

ABOVE: Christina loves fashion and two of her favorite designers are Domenico Dolce and Stefano Gabbana. "Christina is the perfect model for our D&G collection," says Dolce.

OPPOSITE: Christina's advice to her fans: "Just follow your heart, know what you want, and go for it!"

O f course, Christina was born beautiful, but to keep her look fresh and terrific, she doesn't rely on a genie in a bottle—instead, she uses good old common sense.

CLOTHES

On stage, Christina is up for all kinds of wild and interesting clothes. But in her off-camera life, Christina favors casual clothes in soft colors. "I'm definitely a jeans and T-shirt girl," she says. "I love being comfortable."

EYES

Christina keeps her daytime eye makeup very simple, relying on light, neutral shades. Just a touch of mascara is all she needs to make her blue eyes look beautiful. And instead of giving her eyes one heavy coating of mascara, which can look clumpy, Christina lightly applies two coats. She has also learned from top makeup artists to brush her brows with a tiny brush to keep them looking groomed.

At night, Christina opts for a darker, sexier look. Clinique Quickliner in New Black does the trick. On her eyelids, Christina favors a pale peach frosted shadow and a chestnut brown cream shadow in the crease to make those baby blues pop.

SKIN

Christina likes a very light base of foundation over her perfect skin, since too much foundation can look cakey and fake and it will also clog pores. Christina

ABOVE: "Christina is already a pretty girl," says her makeup artist. "Most of the time, all she needs is a little eye shadow."

OPPOSITE: "I'm really a deep thinker," Christina says. "It's weird. Sometimes I'll have daydreams of just floating and changing my body into all these different shapes, like a cloud but more beautiful, and flying around the world like an angel, hovering and watching people."

favors oil-free foundations—especially when she knows she'll be spending a lot of time under hot studio lights, which can make her skin too shiny and greasy-looking. Sometimes she just likes to use a bronzer like Prescriptives Sunshine Bronzing Gel.

CHEEKS

Most of the time Christina's skin is so perfect, she can easily make it without blush, but on special occasions just a hint of color will do. On one recent photo shoot Christina loved the look she got when the makeup artist mixed Prescriptives Sunsheen Bronzing Gel with Bonne Bell's Gel Bronze in extra dark and stroked it all over Christina's face to give her a healthy look. Then she dusted a light touch of Christian Dior Natural Rose pale matte pink blush on the apples of her cheeks. It was just enough of a rosy glow for the camera to grab her dynamic looks.

LIPS

Christina's big beautiful lips are one of her most attractive features. She favors light colors like translucent pinks. Often, Christina will line her lips with a neutral-colored

pencil and then just apply a sheer coat of lip gloss over that. Christina also uses products with SPF protection to keep her lips looking healthy as well as beautiful.

NAILS

The one thing Christina really likes to spend a lot of her beauty bucks (and time) on is her nails. She favors French manicures to keep her hands looking marvelous. A lot of the time, she'll have her nails painted a shade of hot pink and then add the French-style white tips on top of that. It's what gives the girl a style all her own.

DIET

Even though she looks a lot taller, Christina is actually a very tiny girl. She's only 5 feet, 2 inches (157.5cm) tall, and her weight usually hovers around 100 pounds (45.4kg). The one thing she doesn't do to keep her great figure is diet. In fact, she's addicted to junk food! "Christina is naturally thin," says one stylist who has worked with her. "But she stays in amazing shape through all the dancing she does."

LEFT: *Christina had a great time serving a Thanksgiving dinner at the Harley Davidson Cafe in New York City.*

OPPOSITE: *"Every day is different," Christina says of her life now. "A lot of back-to-back interviews and rehearsals for whatever. I'm constantly on the go. If it's not that, it's plane flights. I'm living out of suitcases."*

Boys, Boys, Boys

Like most teenage girls, Christina Aguilera is into guys in a big way. Of course, every guy in the world wants to get close to her, too. It's a problem this blue-eyed blonde is willing to deal with—even if she's suddenly found she's the most popular girl just about everywhere she goes. Christina says she has to approach the entire situation of dating with a lot of humor these days.

"Maybe guys just want to date me because I'm famous," she laughs. "It's hard to have both a career and a boyfriend. I'm single. I've no time for guys. If I met someone I was attracted to, who knows? Perhaps I'll have time for a little fling."

Don't look for Christina to be hooking up with a member of the Backstreet Boys or 'N Sync. She's more likely to be spotted with a guy who's a little rough around the edges. "I go more for the rock 'n' roll type of guys. I'm not that into dating boy groups," she explains.

"I had a long-running crush on Mark McGrath of Sugar Ray, but that's over. He's totally cute, but his whole presence is arrogance. Plus I'm not diggin' the way he's

Christina says one of the strangest things about being famous is the reaction she now gets from guys. "I've heard a few guys going 'Oh my God!' when they see me."

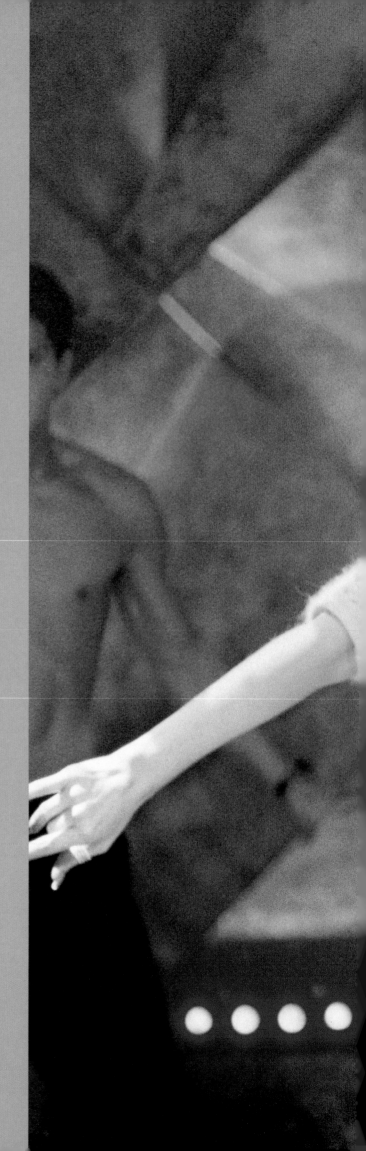

looking right now. Fred Durst is cute, but he doesn't make the crush list.

"All I have are fantasies right now, because I don't have any free time. But I do want to date a performer. It's important to me that I date someone who understands my schedule. Coming out of high school, I've had it with these guys who don't get it."

Christina's tastes in men are constantly changing too. Last year she said, "Robbie Williams and I would make a great couple." She's since been linked (at least in the gossip columns) to MTV's Carson Daly and Limp Bizkit's Fred Durst. Next, she said she was totally into her Super Bowl costar Enrique Iglesias, who held her hand during their performance together. "He is so-o-o good looking," Christina says. "He's a really excellent artist too. I'm a big fan."

Christina jokes that she has an entire routine worked out to attract Enrique's attention. "I'd use my seductive walk," she laughs. "Lots of glancing over and looking back again. I have this little walk and my dancers love it."

So even without a regular boyfriend, Christina is definitely enjoying every moment of being a swinging single. "There are people around me that are definitely giving me love and support and affection, but right now, my career is my boyfriend," she says.

So what does a guy need to know if he's going to rub Christina the right way? "I'm a perfectionist. I'm a control freak," she says. "And I have a problem being totally open and vulnerable, but once I get to know someone that wall gets broken down."

"People are starting to realize that Britney and I are two completely different artists," says Christina of Britney Spears. Christina has her own style.

LEFT: Christina was named best new artist by the readers of Teen People magazine. "With all the new talented artists out there, I am honored to have been chosen number one by the readers and fans," she says.

OPPOSITE: "It's really important to remember that no matter how bad a situation is, it's your outlook that will either get you through or mean that you will fail," Christina says. "At the end of the day, it's down to you to take the chances that are open for you."

CHAPTER SIX

Take the Christina Quiz

"It was all about the live performances and playing these venues and hearing the kids. I mean, hearing kids sing back to me my own lyrics is something I've always wanted."

Christina couldn't resist jumping on one of the motorcycles at the Harley Davidson Cafe in New York City. She was there working on the annual Thanksgiving Feast hosted by the Big Brothers and Sisters.

If you're a fan of Christina, you probably think you know everything there is to know about this up-and-coming diva. Now's the time to put your Aguilera I.Q. to the test!

1. Christina lived in Texas, Japan, and New Jersey when she was little because her father did what for a living?

a. He was a doctor

b. He was a dentist

c. He was in the army

d. He was a rock star

2. What is Christina's favorite food?

a. Pizza

b. Sushi

c. Peanut Butter

d. Fast food

3. Christina has how many siblings?

a. One

b. Two

c. Three

d. Four

4. Whom did Christina always look up to when she was younger?

a. Eleanor Roosevelt

b. Keri Russell

c. Tina Turner

d. Michael Jackson

"When I sing 'Rub me the right way,' people should translate that as 'Treat me the right way.' "

5. Christina's debut album entered the charts at number one. Whom did she bump out of the top slot?

a. Britney Spears

b. Madonna

c. Backstreet Boys

d. Puff Daddy

6. When Christina was eight years old, what did she sing on *Star Search?*

a. "Me and Bobby McGee"

b. "At Last"

c. "The Greatest Love of All"

d. "I Will Always Love You"

7. For what Disney film did Christina record the song "Reflection"?

a. Mulan

b. The Lion King

c. Hercules

d. Tarzan

8. Christina had a crush on which pop star?

a. Kevin Richardson of the Backstreet Boys

b. Mark McGrath of Sugar Ray

c. Flea of the Red Hot Chili Peppers

d. JC Chasez of 'N Sync

9. Where was the video for "Genie in a Bottle" shot?

a. Paris

b. Malibu

c. Prague

d. Los Angeles

10. What kind of a car is Christina thinking about buying?

a. New Beetle

b. Bronco

c. Corvette

d. Porsche

11. Who runs Christina's fan club?

a. Britney Spears

b. Her mom

c. Her sister

d. Her dog

12. What is Christina's secret fear?

a. Spiders

b. Heights

c. The dark

d. Aliens

13. Whom does Christina consider her "Genie in a Bottle"?

a. Her vocal coach

b. Her mom

c. Her granny

d. Her sister

Christina loves getting gifts from her fans and remembers the days when she was a part of the audience. "I would get those pinups in the magazines and put them up on my wall," she remembers. "I completely adored Whitney Houston, I just really felt the whole soul thing. And she is such a chameleon, always reinventing herself. I look up to her for that."

14. Christina is often compared to:

a. Shania Twain

b. Aretha Franklin

c. Madonna

d. Mariah Carey

15. Which of the following artists was also nominated for the Best New Artist Grammy in 2000, which Christina won?

a. Mandy Moore

b. Britney Spears

c. Jessica Simpson

d. LFO

16. What is Christina's ethnic heritage?

a. Italian and German

b. Spanish and French

c. Ecuadoran and Irish

d. Portuguese and Irish

17. Christina's mother plays what instruments?

a. Piano and flute

b. Cello and violin

c. Viola and flute

d. Violin and piano

18. Christina's favorite fashion designer is:

a. Gianni Versace

b. Tommy Hilfiger

c. Dolce & Gabbana

d. Donna Karan

19. Christina's star sign is:

a. Sagittarius

b. Scorpio

c. Pisces

d. Cancer

20. Where was Christina born?

a. Albany, New York

b. Brooklyn, New York

c. Staten Island, New York

d. Wexford, Pennsylvania

"I'm a total night person,"
Christina says. "Even if I
wasn't working late or touring,
I'd be staying up anyway!"

BIBLIOGRAPHY

Anderman, John "Aguilera Shows Her Potential to Be More Than Just Marketing." *Boston Globe*. (September 10, 1999): 76.

Aquilante, Dan. "Dreaming of Genie." *New York Post*. (August 24, 1999): 53.

Bozza, Anthony. "The Christina Aguilera Story." *Rolling Stone*. (October 28, 1999): 55–58.

"Christina Aguilera." *Teen People*. (August 1999): 81.

"Christina Aguilera." *Jump* (September 1999): 12.

"Christina Aguilera in D&G." *Teen People*. (November 1999): 12.

Collis, Clark. "Christina Aguilera." *Q*. (January 2000): 22.

Dominguez, Robert. "What a young star wants." *New York Daily News*. (January 16, 2000): 15.

Ehrman, Marc. "The Magic Touch." *Teen People*. (October 1999): 34–36.

"From Mickey…To Genie." *YM* (August 1999): 8.

Graham, Jefferson. "Wishes Come True." *USA Today*. (March 10, 2000): 8E.

Gregory, Sophfronia Scott. "Uncorking the Genie." *People*. (September 27, 1999): 75–76.

Hoffman, Bill. "Pop Star Aguilera's French Diss." *New York Post*. (February 22, 2000): 51.

"How Much Do We Love Christina Aguilera? Let Us Count The Ways…" *YM*. (February 2000): 71–75.

Jamison, Laura. "Heavy Weight." *Teen People*. (January 2000): 93–96.

Johnson, Beth. "Christina's World."

Entertainment Weekly. (Fall 1999): 126.

Lewin, Kevin. "Christina Aguilera: The Truth About Love, Men and That Feud With Britney." *The National Enquirer*. (March 25, 2000): 47.

Martinez, Jose. "Christina Aguilera: 'I'm So Jazzed!'" *Latin Scene*. (January 2000): 52.

Mendez, Juan. "Unbottled and Unleashed." *Latina*. (January 1999): 78–82.

Pearson, Jennifer. "Sexy Christina flips for video jock." *Star*. (January 25, 2000): 10.

Pollack, Marc. "Aguilera At Number One." *Chicago Sun Times*. (September 3, 1999): 44.

Sodergren, Rebecca. "The Right Note." *Pittsburgh Post Gazette*. (July 30, 1999): 88.

Thigpen, David E. "Christina's World." *Time*. (August 16, 1999): 25.

Turner, Megan. "Battle of the Bubblegum Divas." *New York Post*. (January 20, 2000): 51.

Valdes-Rodriguez, Alisa. "Conjuring a Hit." *Chicago Sun Times*. (August 20, 1999): 52.

Valdes-Rodriguez, Alisa. "Genie Behind Bottle." *Los Angeles Times*. (July 26, 1999): F7.

Vaziri, Aidin. "Q&A With Christina Aguilera." *San Francisco Chronicle*. (August 22, 1999): 24.

Vigoda, Arlene. "Ex-Mouseketeer a hit in rat race." *USA Today* (July 20, 1999): L4.

Vitrano, Alyssa. "Putting Girl Power Into Pop." *YM*. (January 2000): 75–78.

"Wishin' on a star." *Sugar*. (November 1999): 60–62.

Yow, Elizabeth. "Pure Magic." *YM*. (September 1999): 130.

Christina Aguilera Websites

www.Christina-Aguilera.com
The official site for Christina Aguilera

www.bestchristina.com/
Includes chat, message board, bio, photos and more

www.caguilera.com/
Includes news, photos, articles, lyrics and links

Central.Christina-Aguilera.net
Includes news, photos, biography and more

Christina-a.4mg.com/
Fan site containing biography, pictures, lyrics and more

Christina.mundane.nu/
Includes pictures, bio, articles

Features.yahoo.com/webceleb/aguilera/
Includes music news, photos, and concert reviews

www.geocities.com/avoiceofanangel/
Unofficial fan site

www.geocities.com/hollywood/hills/8002/
Unofficial fan site

www.geocities.com/slayergurly/lyrics.html
Unofficial fan site

www.gurlpges.com/music.christinapage/index.html
Unofficial fan site

www.peeps.com/Christina/
Music News

www.todaysbeat.com/aguilera/
News, pictures, biography, and more

Wallofsound.go.com/artists/christinaguilera/home.html
News, reviews, bio, discography, and more

PHOTO CREDITS

INDEX